ONE NATION FOR ALL
IMMIGRANTS IN THE UNITED STATES

LIFE AS AN IRAQI AMERICAN

ELLEN CREAGER

PowerKiDS press

Published in 2018 by The Rosen Publishing Group, Inc.
29 East 21st Street, New York, NY 10010

Cataloging-in-Publication Data

Names: Creager, Ellen.

Title: Life as an Iraqi American / Ellen Creager.

Description: New York : PowerKids Press, 2018. | Series: One nation for all: immigrants in the United States | Includes index.

Identifiers: LCCN ISBN 9781538323403 (pbk.) | ISBN 9781538322444 (library bound) | ISBN 9781538323410 (6 pack)

Subjects: LCSH: Refugees--Iraq--Juvenile literature. | Immigrants--United States--Juvenile literature.

Classification: LCC HV640.5.I76 C74 2018 | DDC 362.7'791409567--dc23

Developed and produced for Rosen by BlueApple*Works* Inc.
Art Director: T.J. Choleva
Managing Editor for BlueApple*Works*: Melissa McClellan
Designer: Joshua Avramson
Photo Research: Jane Reid
Editor: Marcia Abramson

Photo Credits: cover Tracy Whiteside/Shutterstock title page Jon Bilous /Shutterstock.com; flag Les Cunliffe/Dreamstime; background HorenkO/Shutterstock; p. 4 REUTERS/Alamy Stock Photo; p. 6 Alan Gignoux/Alamy Stock Photo; p. 7 Independent Picture Service/Alamy Stock Photo; p. 8 Serban Bogdan/Shutterstock; p. 11 Killua X/Shutterstock; p. 12 SSGT D. Myles Cullen, USAF/Public Domain; p. 14 Joseph Sohm/Shutterstock.com; p. 17 Josef Hanus /Shutterstock; p. 18 Melih Cevdet Teksen/Shutterstock.com; p. 22 dbimages/Alamy Stock Photo; p. 24 Zurijeta/Shutterstock; p. 26 ton koene/Alamy Stock Photo; p. 29 Basharh/Creative Commons

Manufactured in the United States of America

CPSIA Compliance Information: Batch BW18PK: For Further Information contact Rosen Publishing, New York, New York at 1-800-237-9932.

CONTENTS

U.S. families with roots in the country of Iraq are known as Iraqi Americans.

WHO ARE IRAQI AMERICANS?

Many Iraqi Americans are recent immigrants to the United States. Some are **refugees** who are escaping trouble in their homeland. Other Iraqi Americans can trace their heritage to Iraq because their parents, grandparents, or great grandparents came from there. Many Iraqi American families have been in the United States for several generations.

About 213,000 people born in Iraq live in the United States, according to the 2015 U.S. census. There are large Iraqi American populations in the cities of Detroit, San Diego, and Chicago. Other Iraqi Americans have made their homes in New York, Arizona, Tennessee, and other states.

There are many Iraqi American business owners in the United States. Other Iraqi Americans are artists, doctors, teachers, entertainers, scientists – any profession you can imagine. Iraqi Americans are an integral part of American culture.

Young people often lead the way in helping their families adjust to living in a new country.

Iraqi Americans are of many different ethnicities and faiths. Many Assyrians and Chaldeans have immigrated to the United States. Their homeland is in what is now Iraq and neighboring nations. Most Assyrians and Chaldeans are Christians. Other Iraqi minorities, such as Kurds, Mandaeans, and Jews, have also emigrated from Iraq to the United States. There are also many Muslim Iraqi Americans. **Islam** is the predominant religion in Iraq.

Muslims now make up 97 percent of Iraq's population.

... DID YOU KNOW? ...

Iraqi American Religions

Immigrants from Iraq bring their faith with them. Iraqi Americans may be:

Muslims: Believers follow the teachings of Muhammad. Their holy book is the Koran. The religion, Islam, has two branches. Most Iraqi people are Shia Muslim, while others are Sunni Muslim. The division dates back to a dispute about who should be leader once Muhammad died.

Christians: Christians follow the teachings of Jesus. Their holy book is the Bible. Iraqi American Christians are mostly Catholic Assyrian-Chaldeans. Their traditional language is Aramaic.

Mandaeans: This small minority religion is pacifist (they do not believe in fighting). Their holy book is the Ginza Rabba.

Yazidis: They belong to a group called Kurds, but they are not Muslim like most Kurds. They have their own ancient religion.

Jews: Their Iraqi heritage dates to ancient times. Their holy book, the Babylonian Talmud, was written there. They arrived in the United States mostly in the early and mid-twentieth century.

Iraq's main city is the capital, Baghdad, which has about 6.6 million people.

HISTORY OF IRAQ

The land that is now Iraq has an amazing history that dates back 6,000 years. Located in the Middle East, Iraq spans 169,235 square miles (272,357 km), about the size of the state of California. Iraq has a population of about 38.1 million people.

To the north is the country of Turkey. To the east are the countries of Iran and Kuwait. To the west are the countries of Syria and Jordan. To the south is the country of Saudi Arabia.

Most people of Iraq speak Arabic. Others speak Kurdish, Aramaic, or other languages. Most Iraqis are **Arabs**, but not all.

About 97 percent of the people who live in Iraq practice Islam as of 2015. Nearly 60 percent are Shia and 40 percent are Sunni Muslims. These groups are often in conflict. Iraq's people of minority religions have mostly fled Iraq due to **persecution**.

THE CRADLE OF CIVILIZATION

Iraq was once part of a land called Mesopotamia between the Tigris and Euphrates rivers. The name comes from the Greek for "the land between the rivers." It is one of the most important regions in world history. Known as the "cradle of civilization," it was home to the first civilization. Some even believe the biblical Garden of Eden was there.

Mesopotamia's earliest people, the Sumerians, lived 6,000 years ago. They invented farming, cities, the first writing system, the arch, and even the wheel. A little later, other ancient people, notably the Babylonians, made advances in government, architecture, time measurement, mathematics, and geometry. Our 360-degree circle and our 60-minute hour come from them.

There were constant battles and invasions in this land. Arabs invaded in AD 634 and brought the Muslim religion a period of glory.

In 1258, Mongols from the north invaded, followed by Turks. Turkish rule lasted in Mesopotamia for centuries. Then in the twentieth century, billions of barrels of oil were discovered under the ancient ground. The rest of the world wanted a part of this resource.

Oil is the major export of Iraq, but the country has to import food.

After World War I, Mesopotamia was broken into various nations, one of them Iraq. It was ruled for more than a decade by Britain. Iraq gained independence in 1932, became a republic in 1958, then endured a series of **dictators**. One of the harshest dictators was Saddam Hussein. He took power in 1979 and ruled for 24 years.

Hussein pulled Iraq into three wars. First came a bloody war against neighbor Iran from 1980 to 1988. Nearly 700,000 people died. Then his army invaded a small neighboring country, Kuwait. The United States and other nations came to help Kuwait, fighting Iraq in the short Persian Gulf War in 1991 until Hussein retreated. Finally, in 2003, the United States and other countries invaded Iraq because they thought the country was developing dangerous chemical and nuclear weapons.

Saddam Hussein was tried in 2006 and found guilty of mass murder and other crimes.

They did not find the weapons, but they found Saddam Hussein and put him in jail. He was later put on trial and executed by Iraqi authorities. A new democratic government came in, and people voted for their leaders. But then, instead of making the nation safer, things got worse.

ENDLESS CONFLICT

The Iraq War and U.S. **occupation** lasted eight years. Life in Iraq became dangerous and difficult as the terror group al-Qaeda and Iraq's factions fought both each other and the U.S. and **coalition** forces. The United States withdrew its soldiers from Iraq in 2011, leaving a few hundred soldiers behind. However, there were still U.S. troops in Iraq as of 2017.

The violence did not end. Years of economic problems meant continuing hardships. A terror group called the Islamic State took over parts of northern Iraq. Millions of people lost their homes and had to flee or were killed. Many poured into **displaced persons** camps in neighboring countries. While some families were able to reach safer lands like the United States, many could not.

... DID YOU KNOW? ...

Ancient Iraq Symbols

Ancient Mesopotamia, where Iraq is now, is a place of legend and fact:

Hanging Gardens of Babylon: Once considered one of the Seven Wonders of the Ancient World, the glorious gardens are long gone.

Tower of Babel: In the ancient story, it was a tower constructed in what's now northern Iraq by people who all spoke the same language until God scrambled their speech to many different languages.

Garden of Eden: Ancient story of the origin of the world includes mention that it was near the Tigris and Euphrates Rivers, where Iraq is now.

Ishtar Gate: Built in the sixth century B.C. by King Nebuchadnezzar. Portions of the blue tile gate were unearthed in the twentieth century and moved to a German museum where they are on display.

Immigrants can be sworn in as U.S. citizens after they pass a test on history, civics, and the English language.

COMING TO AMERICA

For nearly 120 years, people from what is now Iraq have been coming to America.

One of the earliest groups was the Oussani family. They were Chaldean Christians. They came to the United States in the 1890s from Baghdad and owned a successful tobacco company and land in New York City. Many Assyrians emigrated from Iraq to Chicago in the early 1900s, starting a **vibrant** community there. Some Muslim professionals came to the United States for work, bringing their families. Some Jewish families also came from Baghdad and the historical Babylon region to New York City. By the 1950s, nearly all Jews left Iraq due to **discrimination**. Most went to the new country of Israel, but some came to the United States, settling in southern California and New York.

Still, immigration from Iraq and certain other nations was highly restricted before 1965. The United States had strict **quotas** limiting how many people could come to America. When the Immigration and Nationality Act of 1965 passed, more doors opened.

Starting in the early 1970s, a wave of Assyrian-Chaldean Christians arrived. They settled in Chicago and Detroit. They were mostly business people. Chaldean churches, restaurants, and grocery stores soon provided a comfortable environment for them.

That feeling of belonging was important, because there weren't many Iraq-born people in the United States in the twentieth century. In 1980, only 32,000 immigrants born in Iraq lived in the United States. By 2007 that number jumped to 102,000. By 2015, the number swelled to 215,000, according to U.S. census data.

Wars and conflict in Iraq caused this increase in immigration. The Persian Gulf War in 1991 brought violence and conflict to the country. Many of Iraq's minorities started leaving for safer lands. Then in 2003, the Iraq War began. Up to 7 million Iraqis fled the country.

... DID YOU KNOW? ...

Statue of Liberty's Torch

The stately Statue of Liberty is the symbol of freedom for immigrants to America. Millions passed by her as they arrived in New York City's harbor by boat in the late 1800s and early 1900s.

A gift of the French government in 1886, her surface is made of thin sheets of copper that have turned greenish-gray over the decades. An inscription on her podium has the famous lines, "Give me your tired, your poor, your huddled masses yearning to break free."

Next to the statue is Ellis Island. It is now a museum, but it processed 12 million immigrants into the United States before it closed in 1954.

Today's arriving immigrants from Iraq may not sail past the Statue of Liberty by boat, but they may be lucky enough to catch a glimpse of her if they fly into New York City on a plane.

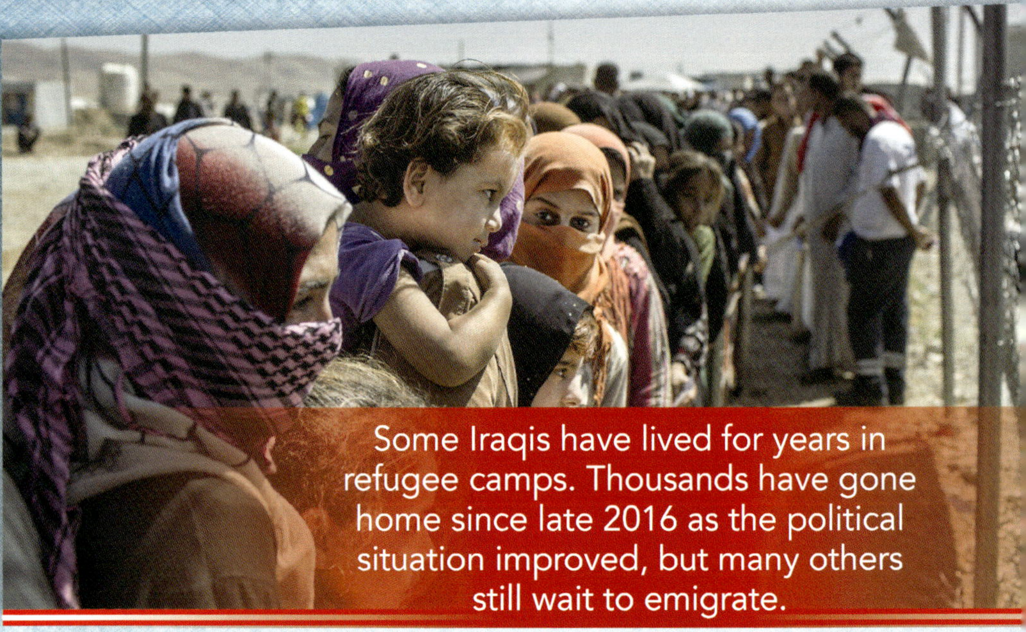

Some Iraqis have lived for years in refugee camps. Thousands have gone home since late 2016 as the political situation improved, but many others still wait to emigrate.

Some people fleeing Iraq lost everything. Families took what they could, moving to cities or refugee camps in the Kurdish region of far northern Iraq or to Turkey, Jordan, Lebanon, or Syria.

In 2007, only 1,608 people born in Iraq came to the United States as refugees. In 2008, 13,823 did, according to U.S. government figures. By 2015, 21,107 people born in Iraq were admitted as permanent residents of the United States. Nearly all of them – 19,000 – were refugees. About one-third of these immigrants were children. They were also far more likely than previous immigrants to have spent time in crowded refugee camps. They were coming not directly from Iraq, but from those camps.

DID YOU KNOW?

Popular Iraqi Foods

Kebabs: beef or lamb, or both, pressed onto skewers and grilled

Masgouf: grilled fresh fish with tamarind and turmeric spices

Hummus: dip made of chickpeas

Fattoush: salad made with pita chips and seasoned with mint and sumac

Turshi: pickled vegetables

Samoon: Iraqi flatbread

Yalanchi: tomatoes stuffed with rice

Again, these new immigrants tended to settle in cities where other Iraqi immigrants already lived. Many Kurdish Muslim people from Iraq's northern territory settled in Nashville, Tennessee, into "Little Kurdistan," which Kurds had established in the 1990s. That created a community of about 15,000 people. Iraq's Assyrian-Chaldean Christians moved mostly to Detroit. Some went on to more recently established communities in San Diego and Phoenix. A minority group called the Mandaeans settled in Detroit and in Worcester, Massachusetts.

Newly arriving Arab Shia Muslim Iraqis have mostly settled in Dearborn, Michigan. It has a thriving Arab American community, including Iraqi American Muslims. Mosques, shops, and community support can help new immigrants feel at home.

Beginning in 2007, the United States began to let in Iraqi immigrants who were English-Arabic translators for the U.S. military in Iraq or who had assisted U.S. forces in some way.

NEW LIFE

Many recent refugee Iraqis have endured a lot of troubles before they arrive. Many have seen war up close. Many have lost family or friends. They may fear authorities after years of violence and stressful living in refugee camps. Many have physical or mental health issues, such as post-traumatic stress disorder.

Other families have been broken up, with some family members allowed to enter the United States and others still waiting an agonizingly long time to see their loved ones again. One group, the Chaldean Community Foundation in Michigan, estimated in 2016 that there was a five- to seven-year wait time to be admitted to the United States, and that 1 million Chaldean people were still waiting.

Many Iraqi families that have been living in the United States for generations have found financial success. For example, families in the large Assyrian-Chaldean community of Detroit today own an estimated 15,000 businesses, from small shops to large companies. Many families live comfortably in suburbs.

Even if they have little, immigrants often send money to help those left behind.

It can be difficult for recent arrivals from Iraq to find financial security. Iraqi immigrants who speak English, are educated, and already have financial resources may adapt more quickly. Iraqi immigrants who don't speak English or have few financial resources often have the hardest time adapting. Resources like the International Rescue Committee, a nonprofit organization, work to help immigrants adjust and succeed in their new home.

Many Iraqi Americans combine aspects of American and Iraqi culture in their daily lives.

LIVING AS AMERICANS

Iraqi immigrants may bring traditions from their home country with them to their new home in the United States. The mixture of American and Iraqi culture is one of the many things that makes the Iraqi American community so vibrant and unique. Here are some of the unique aspects of the Iraqi American community:

★ **Manners count:** Politeness is very important to many Iraqi Americans. Shaking hands, making eye contact, and being a good host are considered polite.

★ **Holidays:** Many Iraqi Americans celebrate American holidays in the United States. They may also celebrate religious holidays. Muslim Iraqi Americans mark Ramadan, a holiday period with a month of fasting from sunup to sundown, then a happy festival at the end called Eid al-Fitr. Christian Iraqi Americans celebrate Christmas, Lent, and Easter. On St. Barbara's Feast Day, they eat a special food called burbara made of boiled wheat, seeds, raisins, and sugar.

Muslim families gather each night of Ramadan to break their fast with a special meal called iftar.

★ **Family life:** Family honor is often important to Iraqi Americans. Education is also highly valued. As in many cultures, Iraqi American parents want to see their children do well in school.

Many Iraqi American families value spending time together. Games such as soccer and backgammon are popular pastimes.

Iraqi Americans may wear clothing styles from their homeland, American clothing, or a combination of the two. Muslim Iraqi American women may wear a head covering called a **hijab**.

Some Iraqi Americans believe in arranged marriages. Others decide to make their own decisions about marriage.

★ **Food:** One of the wonderful ways Iraqi Americans have shaped American society is through food. Many foods from Iraq and other Middle Eastern countries have become part of American culture. Hummus, shawarma, and kebabs are all popular dishes in the United States today. Many Iraqi Americans own or work in restaurants that serve delicious food.

In their own homes, many Muslim Iraqi Americans do not eat pork or drink alcohol, and they stick to meat markets that are halal, meaning that meat is prepared in a special way. Many Iraqi Americans also like strong tea, made with lots of sugar.

Many Iraqi immigrants see their children who are born or raised in America go on to great success.

AMAZING ACHIEVEMENTS

Iraqi Americans have made incredible contributions to the United States and the world. Here are some of the most famous Iraqi Americans who have accomplished great things:

★ **Dr. Mona Hanna-Attisha:** In 2015, Dr. Mona Hanna-Attisha discovered that the tap water in the city of Flint, Michigan, was poisoning the city's children and families with lead. She sounded the alarm. A pediatrician and advocate for children's health, she was born in 1983 in England to scientist parents who had fled Iraq. They emigrated to the United States, and she grew up in Michigan.

★ **Huda Heidi Kattan:** The chief executive of Huda Beauty has millions of followers on social media for her beauty tips. She runs a beauty products company based in Dubai. She was born in 1983 in Oklahoma. Her parents are both from Iraq.

★ **Heather Raffo:** Actress and playwright. She is noted for her one-woman play about Iraqi women, *9 Parts of Desire*. She was born in 1970 in Michigan. Her father is from Baghdad, Iraq.

★ **Wafaa Bilal:** Political artist and associate professor at Tisch School of Arts, New York University. He was born in 1966 in Najaf, Iraq, and emigrated in 1992 to the United States after living in refugee camps. He is known for his edgy art that explores the trauma of conflict.

★ **Alia Shawkat:** Actress on the long-running comedy TV series *Arrested Development*. Her father is from Baghdad. She was born in California in 1989.

★ **Tommy Hanna:** Also known as the rapper Timz, he raps about current events. He was born in 1985 in California. His parents are from Baghdad.

★ **Anisa Mehdi:** Emmy-winning reporter and documentary filmmaker who is a specialist on Islam. She was born in the United States. Her father was from Iraq.

Donny George (Youkhana) worked hard to restore ancient sites and recover items that were looted or damaged during wartime in Iraq.

★ **Donny George (Youkhanna):** The archaeologist helped save treasures as director of the Iraq National Museum after 2003. He immigrated to the United States in 2006. He was born in 1950 in Habbaniyah, Iraq. He died in 2011.

These notable Iraqi Americans have achieved great things in science, medicine, the arts, and other fields. What amazing things will the next generation of Iraqi Americans accomplish?

Glossary

Arab Members of an ethnic group originally from the Arabian Peninsula who now live across the Middle East and northern Africa.

coalition People or countries working together toward a common goal.

dictator A ruler who takes total control.

discrimination Acts of prejudice against someone.

displaced persons People who have been forced to flee their homes or countries.

hijab A head covering worn by some Muslim women.

Islam The name of the religion Muslims practice.

occupation Taking control of an area and ruling it by force.

persecution Treating someone in a cruel and harmful way, often because of religious differences.

quota A certain number.

refugee A person who flees home to seek safety in another place or country.

vibrant Full of life and activity.

For More Information

Further Reading

Ellis, Deborah. *Children of War: Voices of Iraqi Refugees.* Groundwood Books, 2010.

Rodger, Ellen. *A Refugee's Journey from Iraq.* Crabtree Publishing Company, 2017.

Stamaty, Mark Alan. *Alia's Mission: Saving the Books of Iraq.* Dragonfly Books, 2010.

Websites

Due to the changing nature of Internet links, PowerKids Press has developed an online list of websites related to the subject of this book. This site is updated regularly. Please use this link to access the list:
www.powerkidslinks.com/cs/iraqiam

Index